Okki-tokki-un

Action songs for children
chosen by Beatrice Harrop,
Linda Friend and David Gadsby

with PIANO accompaniments
chords for GUITAR
ACTIONS by Linda Friend
and DRAWINGS by David McKee

A & C Black Ltd · London

First published 1976 by A. & C. Black Ltd   35 Bedford Row   London WC1R 4JH   © 1976 A. & C. Black Ltd
Reprinted 1977, 1978, 1979, 1982
ISBN 0 7136 1685 7
A WORDS ONLY edition is also available   ISBN 0 7136 1683 0
Printed in Great Britain by Hollen Street Press Limited, Slough, Berkshire

Contents

1 Heads, shoulders, knees and toes

Heads, shoulders, knees and toes,
  knees and toes,
Heads, shoulders, knees and toes,
  knees and toes
And eyes and ears and mouth and nose,
Heads, shoulders, knees and toes,
  knees and toes.

Music: Based on 'There's a tavern in the town'

eyes and ears and mouth and nose,

C   C7   F

Heads, shoul-ders, knees and toes, knees and toes.

G7   C

ACTIONS

1st time   Sing the song through, touching each part of the body as it is mentioned.

2nd time   Sing the song again, missing out the word 'heads' each time but keeping the action going.

3rd time   This time, don't sing either 'heads' or 'shoulders' but keep the action going.

Keep on repeating the song, missing out one extra item each time – 'knees', then 'toes', then 'eyes', 'ears', 'mouth', 'nose' – until there are no words left and the song is just actions.

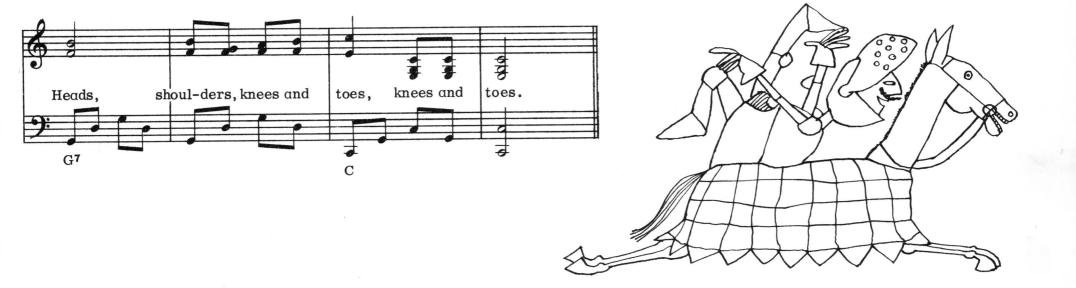

2 Join in the game

Let everyone clap hands with me.
(clap, clap)
It's easy as easy can be.
(clap, clap)
Let everyone join in the game.
(clap, clap)
You'll find that it's always the same.
(clap, clap)

Let everyone whistle with me . . .

Let everyone tap feet with me . . .

Let everyone blink eyes with me . . .

ACTIONS

Carry out the action on the two notes at the end of each line of the verse.

Take it in turns to choose different actions for the others to imitate.

Let ev – ery – one clap hands with me. (clap, clap) It's

eas-y as eas-y can be. (clap, clap) Let ev-ery-one join in the

game. (clap, clap) You'll find that it's al-ways the same. (clap, clap)

3 Everybody do this

Everybody do this,
Do this, do this,
Everybody do this
    Just like me.
Everybody do this,
Do this, do this,
Everybody do this
    Just like me.

ACTIONS

Make up your own actions, as funny as you like.

Keep up the action while singing 'do this' and point to yourself on 'me'.

Words: Mary Miller
Music: American folk song (Hey, Betty Martin)

4 Looby Loo

Here we go Looby Loo,
Here we go Looby Light,
Here we go Looby Loo,
All on a Saturday night.

Put your right hand in,
Put your right hand out,
Shake it a little, a little,
And turn yourself about.
     Here we go Looby Loo . . .

Put your left hand in . . .

Put your right foot in . . . .

Put your left foot in . . .

Put your right hip in . . .

Put your left hip in . . .

Put your big nose in . . .

Put your whole self in . . .

right hand in   left hand in   right foot in   left foot in

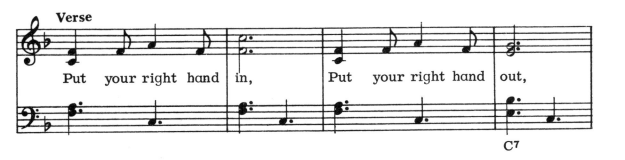

Verse

Put your right hand in, Put your right hand out,

C7

D.C. al Fine

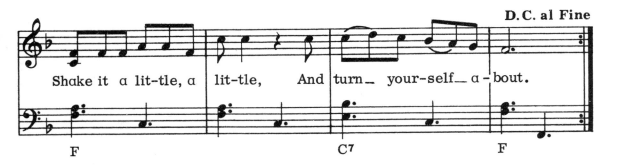

Shake it a lit-tle, a lit-tle, And turn__ your-self__ a-bout.

F   C7   F

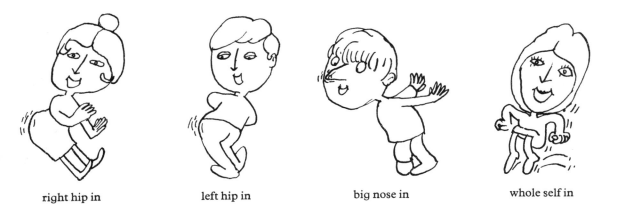

right hip in   left hip in   big nose in   whole self in

ACTIONS

Make a circle.

In the chorus, move round holding hands.

In each verse, mime the actions suggested by the words.

5 The galloping major

Bumpity, bumpity, bumpity, bump,
As if I was riding my charger,
Bumpity, bumpity, bumpity, bump,
As proud as an Indian rajah.
All the girls declare
That I'm a gay old stager.
Hey, hey, clear the way,
Here comes the galloping major!

Words and music: Fred W. Leigh and George Bastow

ACTIONS

Best done sitting down – 'on a charger'.

raise hat

All the girls de - clare ___ That I'm a gay old sta - ger.

F   Bb   Gm   C7

flourish whip

Hey, hey, clear the way, Here comes the gal-lop-ing ma - jor!

F   Bb   C7   F

6 Knees up, Mother Brown

Knees up, Mother Brown! Well!
Knees up, Mother Brown!
Under the table you must go,
Ee-i-ee-i-ee-i-oh!
If I catch you bending,
I'll saw your leg right off.
So, knees up, knees up!
Don't get the breeze up,
Knees up, Mother Brown! Ooh!

Knees up, Mother Brown! Well!
Knees up, Mother Brown!
Come along, dearie, let it go,
Ee-i-ee-i-ee-i-oh!
It's yer blooming birthday,
Let's wake up all the town!
So, knees up, knees up!
Don't get the breeze up,
Knees up, Mother Brown! Ooh!

Words and music: Harris Weston and Bert Lee

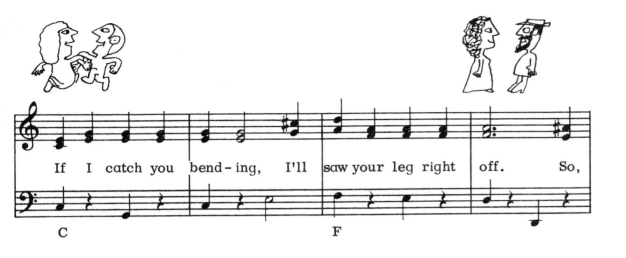

If I catch you bend-ing, I'll saw your leg right off. So,

C   F

ACTIONS

Face a partner.

Three running steps towards partner; on fourth beat, shout 'Well!', slightly bending knees and holding trousers or skirt.

Four running steps back.

Eight hops, twice on each foot beginning with right, holding out alternate arms (right first) to partner, palm up.

Link right arms with partner, turn round and return to place (8 steps).

Hop on alternate feet, knees high – four hops on spot, four towards partner, shouting 'Ooh' on last beat.

knees up, knees up! Don't get the breeze up, Knees up, Moth-er Brown. Ooh!

G7   C

7 Bobbing up and down like this

Sons of the sea,
  Bobbing up and down like this,
Sailing the ocean,
  Bobbing up and down like this.
They may build their ships, my lads,
  Bobbing up and down like this,
But they can't beat the boys of the Old Brigade,
  Bobbing up and down like this.

Pirates so free,
  Bobbing up and down like this,
Searching the ocean,
  Bobbing up and down like this.
They care naught for wind or rain,
  Bobbing up and down like this,
For they rob the gold on the Spanish Main,
  Bobbing up and down like this.

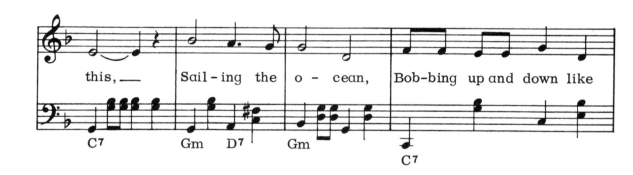

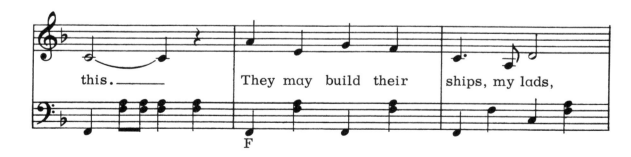

Words and music: Freely adapted from 'Sons of the Sea'
by Felix McGlennon

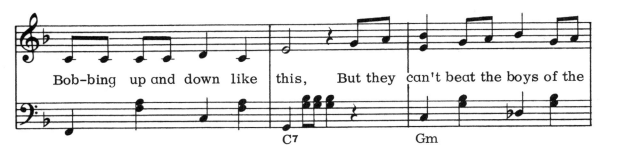

Bob-bing up and down like this, But they can't beat the boys of the

ACTIONS

Bob up and down whenever the words 'bobbing up and down' are sung.

Old Brig-ade, Bob-bing up and down like this.

8 The prehistoric animal brigade

Listen to the chorus
Of the brontosaurus
And the stegosaurus
Down by the swamp.

Along comes the dinosaur,
Making such a loud roar,
Thumping with his feet
And going stomp, stomp, stomp.

Pterodactyl flapping,
Long beak clacking,
Big teeth snapping,
Down from the tree.

Here's a woolly mammoth,
Tusks all curly,
Joins the hurly burly,
Oh dear me!

What a noise!
It's the boys
Of the prehistoric animal brigade!

Words and music: M. L. Reeve

Pter-o-dac-tyl flap-ping, Long beak clack-ing, Big teeth snap-ping,

A

Down from the tree. Here's a wool-ly mam-moth, Tusks all cur-ly,

E 7   A   B♭

Chorus

Joins the hur-ly bur-ly, Oh dear me! What a noise! It's the

B♭

D.S. al Fine   **Fine**

boys Of the pre-his-tor-ic An-i-mal Bri-gade! What a -gade!

F7   B♭   B♭

ACTIONS

As the chorus is repeated, stamp feet and clap in time to music, stopping all noise sharply on final chord.

N.B. In the chorus, on the words 'What a noise! It's the boys', the lower note of the top two notes can be sung as the melody.

9 Eat brown bread

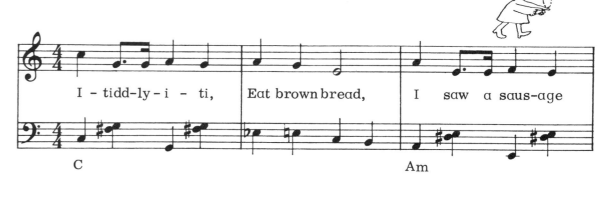

I – tiddly – i – ti,
Eat brown bread.
I saw a sausage
Fall down dead.
Up jumped a saveloy
And bashed him on the head.
I – tiddly – i – ti,
— BROWN BREAD!

ACTIONS

Mime sausage shape, then mime falling down, jumping up, bashing on head.

Finish with two loud claps on 'BROWN BREAD'.

Music: Gail Smart

10 This way, that-a way

When I was a little boy, little ol' little boy,
When I was a little boy five years old,
Daddy came and got me, came and got me,
Daddy didn't scold me, I've been told.

    Ha-ha! this-a way,
    Ha-ha! that-a way,
    Ha-ha! this-a way,
    Then, oh then.

I went into school there, little ol' school
    there,
Went into the school there, school so old;
Learned the Golden Rule there, little ol' rule
    there,
Learned the Golden Rule there, I've been told.

Learned my lesson, little ol' lesson,
Learned my lesson like I was told.
Wasn't that a blessing, little ol' blessing?
Learned my lesson at five years old.

Met my teacher, little ol' teacher,
Met my teacher, he didn't scold;
Said 'I'm glad ter meetcha, meetcha, meetcha,'
Said 'I'm glad ter meetcha,' I've been told.

ACTIONS
These are in the chorus only: someone sings the verses
and everyone joins in the chorus, with actions.

Words and music: American traditional arranged
by Elizabeth Poston

11 The animal fair

I went to the animal fair,
The birds and the beasts were there,
The gay baboon by the light of the moon
Was combing his auburn hair.
The monkey fell out of his bunk,
And slid down the elephant's trunk,
The elephant sneezed and fell on his knees,
And that was the end of the monkey, monkey,
    monkey, monkey,
Monkey, monkey, monkey, monkey, monk.

ACTIONS

The song begins and ends with rhythmic clapping, alternately own hands and partner's hands.

The sound effects come best at the end of the line.

12 Miss Mary Mac

Miss Mary Mac, Mac, Mac,
All dressed in black, black, black,
With silver buttons, buttons, buttons,
All down her back, back, back.
　　She cannot read, read, read,
　　She cannot write, write, write,
　　But she can smoke, smoke, smoke,
　　Her father's pipe, pipe, pipe.
She asked her mother, mother, mother,
For fifty pence, pence, pence,
To see the elephant, elephant, elephant
Climb up the fence, fence, fence.
　　He climbed so high, high, high,
　　He reached the sky, sky, sky,
　　And never came back, back, back,
　　Till the fourth of July,-ly,-ly.
She went upstairs, stairs, stairs,
And bumped her head, head, head,
And now she's DEAD.

repeat four more times

last verse

stairs,   stairs,   stairs, And bumped her

F   C7

loud clap – silence

head,   head,   head, And now she's DEAD.

F   C7   F

ACTIONS

Face a partner, standing or sitting, and repeat the eight actions over and over, one to each beat.

OR do the actions while moving round sideways in a circle, clapping the hands of the person at each side on beats 4, 6 and 8.

OR have two facing circles, moving in opposite directions.

13 The wild oak tree

Love grows under the wild oak tree,
Sugar melts like candy,
Top of the mountain shines like gold
And you kiss your little fella sorta handy.

Dreams, dreams, sweet dreams,
Under the wild oak tree-ee,
Dreams, dreams, sweet dreams,
One for you and me! So!

Love grows under the wild oak tree,
Sugar melts like candy,
Top of the mountain shines like gold
And you kiss your little fella sorta handy.

Words and music: North American

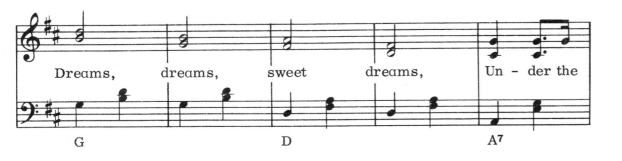

Dreams, dreams, sweet dreams, Un – der the

G   D   A7

wild oak tree – ee, Dreams, dreams, sweet

D   G   D

D.C. al Fine

dreams, One for you and me! So!

E7   A   A7

ACTIONS

Keep these going in time to the music. The knee slaps, hand claps, finger snaps and hand rolling continue through the song.

14 Someone's in the kitchen with Dinah

Someone's in the kitchen with Dinah,
Someone's in the kitchen, I know, I know,
Someone's in the kitchen with Dinah,
Strumming on the old banjo.

Fee, fie, fiddle-ee-i-o,
Fee, fie, fiddle-ee-i-o,
Fee, fie, fiddle-ee-i-o,
Strumming on the old banjo.

Fee, plonk, fie, plonk,
    fiddle-ee-i-o, plonk,
Fee, plonk, fie, plonk,
    fiddle-ee-i-o, plonk,
Fee, plonk, fie, plonk,
    fiddle-ee-i-o, plonk,
Strumming on the old banjo.

Someone's in the kitchen with Dinah,
Someone's in the kitchen, I know, I know,
Someone's in the kitchen with Dinah,
Strumming on the old banjo.

-o, Fee, fie, fid-dle-ee-i - o, Strum-ming on the old ban-jo.

F   Bb   C7   F

ACTIONS

Key words (fee, fie, fiddle-ee-i-o, plonk) show when the playing of an instrument is mimed. 'Fee' means flute, 'fie' means clarinet, 'fiddle-ee-i-o' means violin, 'plonk' means drum.

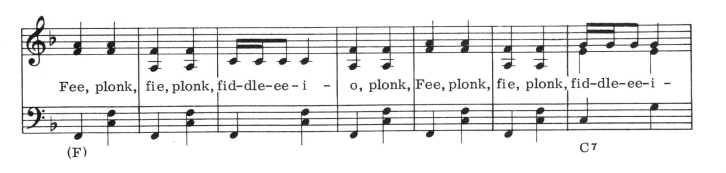

Fee, plonk, fie, plonk, fid-dle-ee-i - o, plonk, Fee, plonk, fie, plonk, fid-dle-ee-i -

(F)   C7

Fee (flute)

plonk (drum)

fie (clarinet)

plonk

D.C. al Fine

-o, plonk, Fee, plonk, fie, plonk, fid-dle-ee-i - o, plonk, Strumming on the old ban-jo.

F   Bb   C7   F

fiddle-ee-i-o (violin)

plonk

15 Okki-tokki-unga

This is the story of an eskimo boy who goes on a seal hunt to win a bride.

Chorus

Ok-ki-tok-ki-un-ga, Ok-ki-tok-ki-un-ga,

D   A7

Hey, Mis-sa Day, Mis-sa Doh, Mis-sa Day,

D   A7   D

Ok-ki-tok-ki-un-ga, Ok-ki-tok-ki-un-ga,

A7

Fine

Hey, Mis-sa Day, Mis-sa Doh, Mis-sa Day.

D   A7   D

CHORUS ACTIONS

Swing folded arms from side to side on each beat.

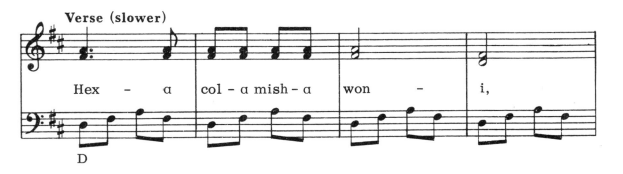

Verse (slower)

Hex - a col-a mish-a won - i,

D

Hex - a col-a mish-a won - i,

A⁷

D.C. al Fine

Hex - a col-a mish-a won - i.

D

The eskimo boy's adventures are mimed as the verses are sung (words of each verse are the same).

Sing the song thus:

Chorus

Verse 1  looks all round in vain for seal

Chorus

Verse 2  sees seal and harpoons it

Chorus

Verse 3  drags seal into his kayak

Chorus

Verse 4 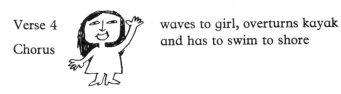 waves to girl, overturns kayak and has to swim to shore

Chorus

16 'Neath the lilacs

She sat 'neath the lilacs and played her guitar,
    Played her guitar, played her guitar,
She sat 'neath the lilacs and played her guitar,
    Played her guitar.

    Um ching-a ching-a, um ching-a ching-a,
    Um ching, ching, ching.

He sat down beside her and smoked his cigar . . .

He said that he loved her but oh, how he lied . . .

She said she believed him but oh, how she sighed . . .

They were to be married but she up and died . . .

He went to her funeral but just for the ride . . .

He sat on her tombstone and laughed till he died . . .

She went up to heaven and flip-flap she flied . . .

He went to the other place and frizzled and fried . . .

The moral of this story is : Don't tell a lie . . .

Or you too may perish and frizzle and fry . . .

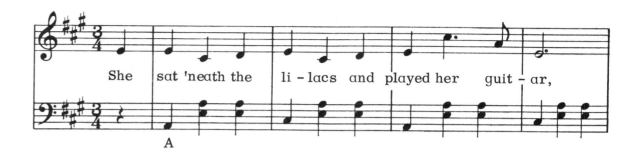

played her guitar   smoked his cigar   oh, how he lied!   oh, how she sighed!

li-lacs and played her guit-ar, Played her guit-ar-ar-ar-

D   E7   A

ACTIONS

Mime actions to suit the repeated phrases in each verse.

'Up and died' can be mimed by raising the arms sideways on 'up' and lowering them on 'died'.

'Frizzled and fried' can be mimed by pointing down on 'frizzled' and mopping forehead on 'fried'.

-ar.   Um ching-a ching-a,   um   ching-a ching-a,   Um ching ching ching.

E7   A

up and died

just for the ride

laughed till he died

flip flap she flied

frizzled and fried

don't tell a lie

17 Miss Polly

Miss Polly had a dolly
Who was sick, sick, sick,
So she 'phoned for the doctor
To be quick, quick, quick.
The doctor came
With his bag and his hat,
And he rapped at the door
With a rat-tat-tat.

He looked at the dolly
And he shook his head.
Then he said, 'Miss Polly,
Put her straight to bed.'
He wrote on a paper
For a pill, pill, pill;
'I'll be back in the morning
With my bill, bill, bill.'

rock arms
from side to side

Words: From an old English rhyme

doc - tor came_ with his bag and his hat, And he

C7

rapped_ at the door_ with a rat - tat - tat.

F   C7   F

ACTIONS

Mime the story as you sing it. Actions for the second verse are suggested below.

shook his head

wrote on a paper

straight to bed

I'll be back

c

18 The three bears

When Goldilocks went to the house of the bears,
Oh, what did her blue eyes see?
  A bowl that was huge,
  A bowl that was small,
  And a bowl that was tiny, and that was all,
  She counted them, one, two, three.

When Goldilocks went to the house of the bears,
Oh, what did her blue eyes see?
  A chair that was huge . . .

When Goldilocks went to the house of the bears,
Oh, what did her blue eyes see?
  A bed that was huge . . .

When Goldilocks ran from the house of the bears,
Oh, what did her blue eyes see?
  A bear that was huge,
  A bear that was small,
  And a bear that was tiny, and that was all,
  They growled at her, grr, grr, grr.

Words: Carolyn Sherwin Bailey
Music: English traditional

bowl that was tin - y and that was all, She

A⁷   D

count-ed them, one, two, three._____

A⁷   Ⓓ   Ⓐ⁷   Ⓓ

a chair that was huge

a chair that was small

a chair that was tiny

a bed that was huge

a bed that was small

a bed that was tiny

a bear that was huge

a bear that was small

a bear that was tiny

ACTIONS

Make your actions suit the words.

Growl fiercely on the last three beats of the last verse.

Yr 2. Tuned Perc.
Yr 1. Untuned Perc.

19 After the ball was over

After the ball was over,
She took out her glass eye,
Put her false teeth in water,
Shook from her hair the dye.
Kicked her cork leg in the corner,
Stripped off her false nails and all,
Then what was left went to bye-byes,
After the ball.

Music: Chas K. Harris

Kicked her cork leg in the cor - ner,

C⁷   F   B♭   F

ACTIONS

Mime the actions in an exaggerated, grotesque manner.

Stripped off her false nails and all, ____ Then what was

D⁷   G   C⁷

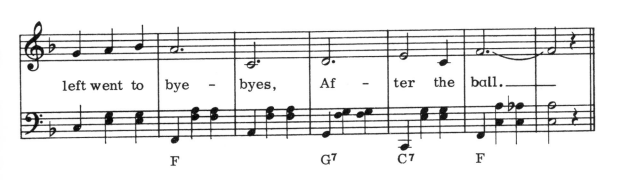

left went to bye - byes, Af - ter the ball. ____

F   G⁷   C⁷   F

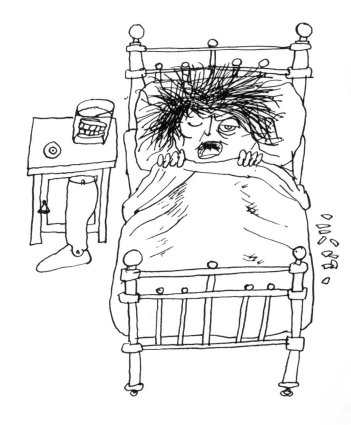

20 The princess

There was a princess long ago,
    Long ago, long ago,
There was a princess long ago,
    Long ago.

And she lived in a big high tower,
    Big high tower, big high tower,
And she lived in a big high tower,
    Big high tower.

One day a bad queen cast a spell . . .

The princess slept for a hundred years . . .

A great big forest grew around . . .

A gallant prince came riding by . . .

He cut the trees down with his sword . . .

He took her hand to wake her up . . .

So everybody's happy now . . .

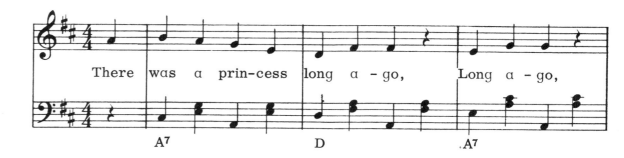

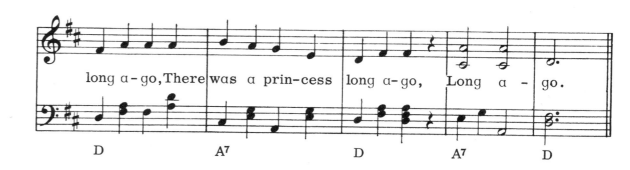

ACTIONS

Mime the story, suiting your actions to the words. You can do these on your own or in a group with three people taking the parts of the princess, queen and prince.

21 Old Roger

Old Roger is dead and he lies in his grave,
    Lies in his grave, lies in his grave,
Old Roger is dead and he lies in his grave,
    Heigh-ho, lies in his grave.

They planted an apple tree over his head,
    Over his head, over his head . . .

The apples got ripe and they all tumbled down . . .

There came an old woman a-picking them up . . .

Old Roger got up and he gave her a poke . . .

This made the old woman go hippety-hop . . .

ACTIONS

Mime the story. You can do this with a partner or as a big group with two people taking the parts of Roger and the old woman.

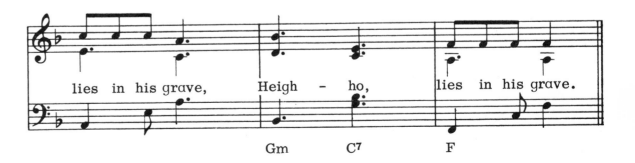

22 Hang on the bell, Nellie

The scene was in the jailhouse
And, if curfew rang that night,
The guy in number thirteen cell
Would go out like a light.
Nell knew her Dad was innocent
And so, poor little 'gel',
Had tied her tender torso
To the clapper of the bell.

Hang on the bell, Nellie,
Hang on the bell.
Your poor Dad is locked
In a cold prison cell.
As you swing to the left
And you swing to the right,
Remember the curfew
Must nevah ring tonight!

Words and music: Tommie Connor, Clive Erard
and Ross Parker

ACTIONS

One person sings the verse and everyone joins in the chorus, with actions.

Chorus

Hang on the bell, Nel-lie, Hang on the bell. Your poor Dad is locked in a

F   Gm   C7

cold pri-son cell. As you swing to the left And you swing to the

F   Gm

right, Re-mem-ber_ the cur-few_ Must ne-vah ring to-night!

C7   F

23 'Neath the spreading chestnut tree

Underneath the spreading chestnut tree,
I loved her and she loved me.
There she used to sit upon my knee,
'Neath the spreading chestnut tree.

There beneath the boughs we used to meet,
All her kisses were so sweet,
All the little birds went tweet, tweet, tweet,
'Neath the spreading chestnut tree.

I said, 'I love you and there ain't no ifs
  nor buts.'
She said, 'I love you,' and the blacksmith
  shouted 'Chestnuts!'

Underneath the spreading chestnut tree,
There she said she'd marry me.
Now you ought to see our family,
'Neath the spreading chestnut tree.

Words and music: Jimmy Kennedy, Tommie Connor
and Hamilton Kennedy

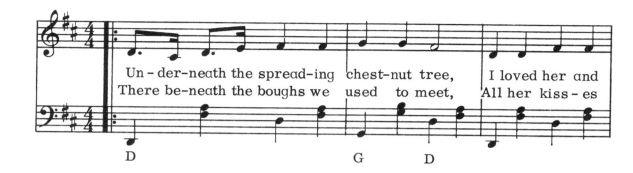

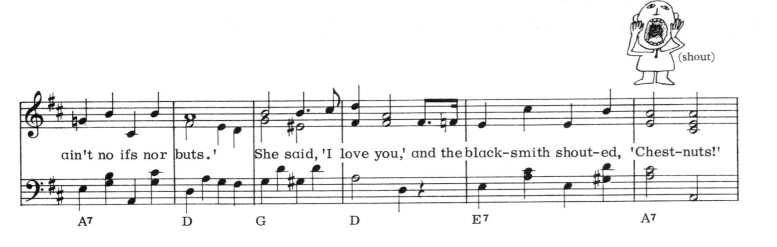

ain't no ifs nor buts.' She said, 'I love you,' and the black-smith shout-ed, 'Chest-nuts!'

A⁷   D   G   D   E⁷   A⁷

ACTIONS

Do these with a partner.

Un - der-neath the spreading chest-nut tree,   There she said she'd mar-ry   me.

D   G   D   A⁷   D

Now you ought to see our fam - i - ly,   'Neath   the spread-ing chest-nut   tree.

G   F♯m   G   D   G   A⁷   D   A⁷   D

24 In a cottage in a wood

In a cottage in a wood,
A little man at the window stood;
Saw a rabbit hopping sore,
Knocking at the door.

'Help me, help me, help me,' he said,
'Or the hunter will shoot me dead!'
'Come, little rabbit, stay with me,
Happy you will be.'

In a cot-tage in a wood, A lit-tle man at the

win-dow stood, Saw a rab-bit, hop-ping sore,

knock on each beat

Knock-ing at the door.

(shout, rather than sing)
'Help me, help me,

help me,' he said,
'Or the hun-ter will shoot me dead!'

F (F)

C7 F

stroke rabbit

'Come, lit-tle rab-bit, stay with me, Hap-py you will be.'

C7 F

ACTIONS

When beckoning and stroking, keep up a rhythmic movement of two beats to a bar.

25 Do your ears hang low?

Do your ears hang low?
Do they wobble to and fro?
Can you tie them in a knot?
Can you tie them in a bow?
Can you toss them over your shoulder
Like a regimental soldier?
Do your ears hang low?

Do your ears hang low? Do they

G

swing arms from side to side

wob - ble to and fro? Can you tie them in a

knot? Can you tie them in a bow? Can you

ACTIONS

Sing the song three times.

1st time Sitting, with average voice and actions.

2nd time Standing, with loud voice and exaggerated actions.

3rd time Sitting, almost whispering and with tiny actions.

toss them o-ver your shoul - der like a reg - i-ment - al

G

sold-ier? Do your ears hang low?_____

D7   G

26 Let's all play at Indians

Let's all play at Indians
'Way out in the west.
I will be the chief
Because I'm braver than the rest!
With my bow and arrow
Go shooting all the day,
Like Indians
That live across the way.

 Oowa – oowa – oowa – oowa . . .

Let's all play at In-dians 'Way out in the west.

D G D G D

chief's headdress down back

pummel chest

I will be the chief Be-cause I'm brav-er than the rest!

Bm E⁷ A⁷

Finish with a rallying cry, flat hand vibrating over open mouth.

With my bow and ar-row Go shoot-ing all the day,   Like In-dians That

D   G   D   G   D

continue ad lib →

live   a-cross the way. Oo-wa, oo-wa, oo-wa, oo-wa, oo-wa, oo-wa, oo-wa

A⁷   D

D

27 Put your finger on your head

Put your finger on your head, on your head,
Put your finger on your head, on your head.
   Put your finger on your head,
    Tell me, is it green or red?
Put your finger on your head, on your head.

Put your finger on your nose, on your nose,
Put your finger on your nose, on your nose.
   Put your finger on your nose,
    You can feel the cold wind blows,
Put your finger on your nose, on your nose.

Put your finger on your cheek, on your cheek,
Put your finger on your cheek, on your cheek.
   Put your finger on your cheek,
    Leave it there about a week,
Put your finger on your cheek, on your cheek.

Put your finger on your ear, on your ear,
Put your finger on your ear, on your ear.
   Put your finger on your ear,
    Leave it there about a year,
Put your finger on your ear, on your ear.

Put your finger on your finger, on your finger,
Put your finger on your finger, on your finger.
   Put your finger on your finger
    And your finger on your finger,
Put your finger on your finger, on your finger.

Words and music: Woody Guthrie

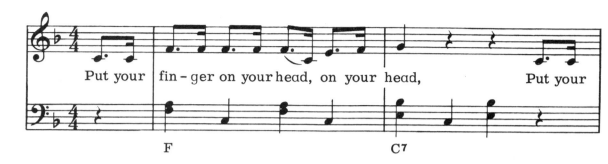

head

nose

fin - ger on your head,   Tell me,   is   it green or red?   Put your

B♭   F

ACTIONS

Keep finger in position all through each verse except the last, where finger changes can be rapid.

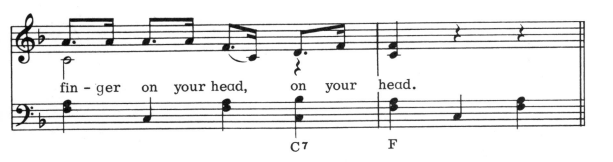

fin - ger   on   your head,   on   your   head.

C7   F

cheek

ear

28 The miner's dream of home

I saw the old homestead and faces I loved,
I saw England's valleys and dells;
I listened with joy, as I did when a boy,
To the sound of the old village bells.
The fire was burning brightly,
'Twas a night that would banish all sin,
For the bells were ringing the Old Year out
And the New Year in.

I saw the old home-stead and fac - es I loved, I
saw Eng-land's val-leys and dells; _____ I list-ened with
joy, as I did when a boy, To the sound of the

Words and music: Will Godwin and Leo Dryden

A miner who has worked abroad for many years dreams one night of home as he re-members it on New Year's Eve.

ACTIONS

When miming bell-ringing, give a good pull downwards on the first beat of each bar.

29 The wise man and the foolish man

The wise man built his house upon the rock,
The wise man built his house upon the rock,
The wise man built his house upon the rock,
    And the rain came tumbling down.
The rain came down and the floods came up,
The rain came down and the floods came up,
The rain came down and the floods came up,
    And the house on the rock stood firm.

The foolish man built his house upon the sand,
The foolish man built his house upon the sand,
The foolish man built his house upon the sand,
    And the rain came tumbling down.
The rain came down and the floods came up,
The rain came down and the floods came up,
The rain came down and the floods came up,
    And the house on the sand fell flat.

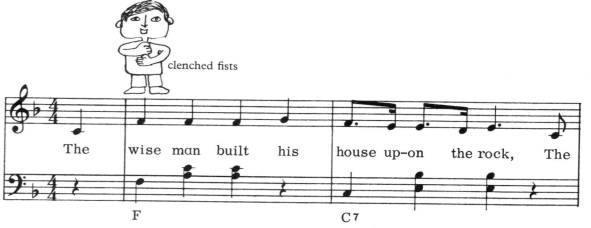

ACTIONS

To indicate the rising water, raise the hands higher each time you sing 'floods'.

In verse 2, to indicate flat sand, hold hands out in front, palms down, and move them out to the side and back again. Finish with a loud clap on 'flat'.

30 Mister Banjo

Look at the dandy there,
Mister Banjo,
Doesn't he put on airs,
Mister Banjo!
  Hat cocked on one side,
  Mister Banjo,
  Walkin' stick in hand,
  Mister Banjo.
Look at the dandy there,
Mister Banjo,
Doesn't he put on airs!

Look at the dandy there . . .
  Boots that go 'krank-krank',
  Mister Banjo,
  Yellow gloves, my eye,
  Mister Banjo.
Look at the dandy there . . .

Look at the dandy there . . .
  Great big diamond ring,
  Mister Banjo,
  Silver watch and chain,
  Mister Banjo.
Look at the dandy there . . .

Words and music: American folk song, Creole

ACTIONS

Try to give your movements an elegant, dandified air.

31 Fishing

Fishing, fishing, down by the sea.
We'll take our fishing rods, you and me.
Sit on the sea-wall, all the long day,
Watching the passing ships far away.
Something is moving, just over there;
See how that big fish jumped into the air?
Is he on your line, is he on mine?
Oh look, I've got him! Isn't he fine!
  Mm – m – m – m – m – m – m – m– m – m.

Words and music: M. L. Reeve

ACTIONS

After singing the song through once, move away and mime the actions as you hum the tune. Or mime the action of fishing as you hum the last four bars.

32 The wheels on the bus

The wheels on the bus go round and round,
    Round and round,
    Round and round,
The wheels on the bus go round and round,
    Over the city streets.

The horn on the bus goes peep, peep, peep . . .

The mums on the bus go chatter, chatter,
    chatter . . .

The dads on the bus go nod, nod, nod . . .

The kids on the bus go wriggle, wriggle,
    wriggle . . .

ACTIONS

Mime the action of the repeated words.

'Chatter' can be mimed by opening and closing thumb and
four straight fingers in a beak-like action.

33 I'm a little teapot

I'm a little teapot, short and stout;
Here is my handle, here is my spout.
When I get all steamed up, then I shout,
'Just tip me over, pour me out.'

I'm a tube of toothpaste on the shelf;
I get so lonely all by myself.
When it comes to night-time, then I shout,
'Just lift my lid off, squeeze me out.'

I'm a little robot, short and square,
I have no toe-nails, I have no hair.
If you want the answer to a sum,
Just press my button, out it comes.

ACTIONS

Make yourself look like a teapot, tube of toothpaste, or robot. Pour, squeeze or press yourself as the words suggest.

Words (first verse) and music: Clarence Kelley and George H. Sanders

34 Cousin Peter

Last evening Cousin Peter came,
Last evening Cousin Peter came,
Last evening Cousin Peter came
    To show that he was here.

He knocked three times upon the door,
He knocked three times upon the door,
He knocked three times upon the door
    To show that he was here.

He wiped his feet upon the mat . . .

He hung his hat upon the hook . . .

He kicked his shoes off one by one . . .

He danced about in stocking-feet . . .

He tossed us up into the air . . .

He played he was a great big bear . . .

He made a bow and said goodbye,
He made a bow and said goodbye,
He made a bow and said goodbye
    To show that he was gone.

ACTIONS

Sing the first verse without actions. From the second verse
onwards, mime the action suggested by the words.

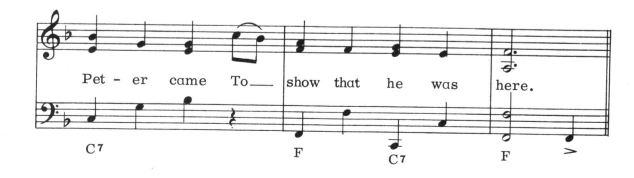

35 One elephant

One elephant went out to play
Upon a spider's web one day.
He found it such enormous fun
That he called for another elephant to come.

ACTIONS

One person takes the first elephant's part and does the actions. On the last line he chooses another 'elephant' to join in.

The song is sung over and over, the second elephant choosing a third, the third a fourth, and so on.

If there is a large number of people, *each* elephant can choose another elephant at the end of each repeat of the verse.

36 The ants go marching

The ants go marching one by one,
    Hurrah, hurrah.
The ants go marching one by one,
    Hurrah, hurrah.
The ants go marching one by one,
The little one stopped to suck his thumb,
And they all went marching down
To the earth to get out of the rain,
    Boom, boom,
To the earth to get out of the rain.

The ants go marching two by two . . .
The little one stopped to do up his shoe

The ants go marching three by three . . .
The little one stopped to climb a tree

The ants go marching four by four . . .
The little one stopped to knock at the door

The ants go marching five by five . . .
The little one stopped to learn to drive

The ants go marching six by six . . .
The little one stopped to pick up sticks

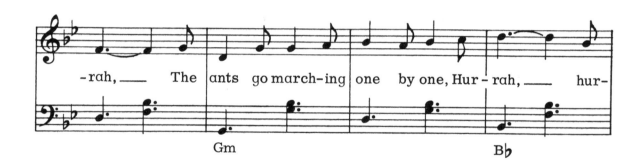

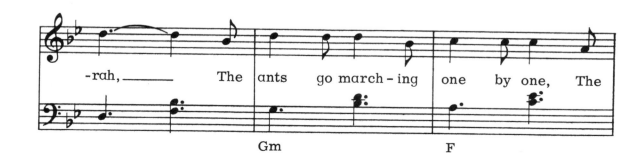

lit-tle one stopped to suck his thumb, And they all went

Gm   D7   Gm   Cm

The ants go marching seven by seven . . .
The little one stopped and went to heaven

The ants go marching eight by eight . . .
The little one stopped to shut the gate

The ants go marching nine by nine . . .
The little one stopped to walk on a line

The ants go marching ten by ten . . .
The little one stopped to say THE END.

march - ing down To the earth to get out of the

Gm   D7   Gm

slap knees

rain, Boom, boom, To the earth to get out of the rain.____

Cm   Gm

ACTIONS

Start each verse by holding up the correct number of fingers.

For the marching action in the second half of the verse, you can use your fingers, walking them along your other arm, the floor, or the table.

E

37 Johnny taps with one hammer

Johnny taps with one hammer,
  one hammer, one hammer,
Johnny taps with one hammer,
Then he taps with two.

Johnny taps with two hammers . . .
Then he taps with three.

Johnny taps with three hammers . . .
Then he taps with four.

Johnny taps with four hammers . . .
Then he taps with five.

Johnny taps with five hammers . . .
Then he goes on strike.

ACTIONS

Add an extra 'hammer' at the end of each verse. After the two fists, add one foot, both feet, and then nodding with the head.

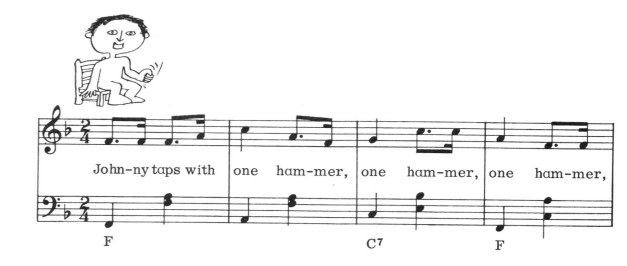

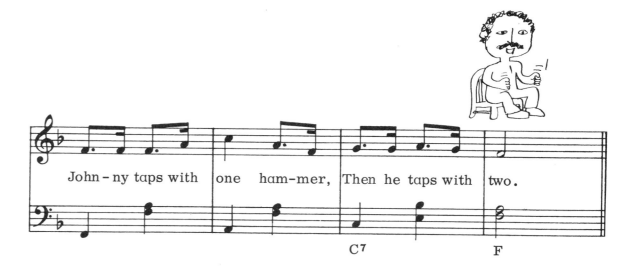

38 Ten fat sausages

Ten fat sausages sizzling in the pan,
Ten fat sausages sizzling in the pan.
One went 'POP!' and another went 'BANG!'
There were eight fat sausages sizzling in the pan.

Eight fat sausages sizzling in the pan,
Eight fat sausages sizzling in the pan.
One went 'POP!' and another went 'BANG!'
There were six fat sausages sizzling in the pan.

Six fat sausages sizzling in the pan . . .

Four fat sausages sizzling in the pan . . .

Two fat sausages sizzling in the pan . . .

ACTIONS

Start each verse by holding up the correct number of
fingers.

39 This old man

This old man, he played one,
He played nick nack on my thumb.
Nick nack paddy whack, give a dog a bone,
This old man came rolling home.

This old man, he played two,
He played nick nack on my shoe . . .

This old man, he played three,
He played nick nack on my knee . . .

This old man, he played four,
He played nick nack on the floor . . .

This old man, he played five,
He played nick nack making a dive . . .

This old man, he played six,
He played nick nack with some sticks . . .

This old man, he played seven,
He played nick nack up in heaven . . .

This old man, he played eight,
He played nick nack on my pate . . .

This old man, he played nine,
He played nick nack on my spine . . .

This old man, he played ten,
He played nick nack once again . . .

ACTIONS

Start each verse by holding up the correct number of fingers.

In the last verse close the fingers on 'once' and open them on 'again'.

40 Ten little squirrels

Ten little squirrels sat on a tree,
The first two said, 'Why, what do we see?'
The next two said, 'A man with a gun.'
The next two said, 'Let's run, let's run.'
The next two said, 'Let's hide in the shade.'
The next two said, 'Why, we're not afraid.'
But BANG went the gun —
    and away they all ran.

Music: Graham C. Westcott

hide   in the shade.'   The   next   two   said, 'Why,   we're   not a-fraid.'   But

G7   C

BANG went the gun,   and a-way they all ran.

Ab   C   C   C   C   G7   C

ACTIONS

Start by holding up all the fingers, then each pair in turn.
Give a good loud clap on 'BANG'.

41 Six little ducks

Six little ducks that I once knew,
Fat ones, skinny ones, they were too;
But the one little duck with the feathers
   on his back,
He ruled the others with his 'Quack, quack, quack!
   quack, quack, quack!'
He ruled the others with his 'Quack, quack, quack!'

Down the river they would go,
Wibble, wabble, wibble, wabble, to and fro;
But the one little duck with the feathers
   on his back . . .

Home from the river they would come,
Wibble, wabble, wibble, wabble, ho-hum-hum;
But the one little duck with the feathers
   on his back . . .

'Quack, quack, quack!   Quack, quack, quack!'

D7   G   D7   G

He   ruled the oth-ers with his   'Quack, quack, quack!'

D7   G

ACTIONS

Make these suit the words of the song.

Move the elbows up and down on each 'quack'.

42 Nicky, knacky, knocky, noo

With my hands on my head,
   What have we here?
This is my main thinker,
   My teacher dear.
Main thinker,
   Nicky, knacky, knocky, noo.
   That's what they taught me
   When I went to school.

With my hands on my head,
   What have we here?
These are my eye blinkers,
   My teacher dear.
Main thinker, eye blinkers,
   Nicky, knacky, knocky, noo.
   That's what they taught me
   When I went to school.

This is my smell boxer

This is my chin wagger

This is my cough chester

This is my bread basket

These are my knee knockers

These are my toe tappers

eye blinkers

smell boxer

chin wagger

ACTIONS

Start each verse with both hands on head. An extra item is added with each verse so that, by the last verse, the hands move progressively down the body from forehead to feet.

Try making up your own rhythmic action for the four beats of 'nicky, knacky, knocky, noo'.

repeat as needed

Main think - er, Nick-y, knack-y, knock-y, noo.

G   D7

That's what they taught me When I went to school.

G

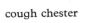

cough chester

bread basket

knee knockers

toe tappers

43 John Brown's baby

John Brown's baby got a cold upon his chest,
John Brown's baby got a cold upon his chest,
John Brown's baby got a cold upon his chest,
So they rubbed it with camphorated oil.

Camphor – amphor – amphor – ated,
Camphor – amphor – amphor – ated,
Camphor – amphor – amphor – ated,
So they rubbed it with camphorated oil.

Chorus

Cam - phor - am-phor-am-phor - at - ed,

Cam - phor - am-phor-am-phor - at - ed,

Cam - phor - am-phor-am-phor - at - ed, So they

rubbed it with cam-phor-at - ed oil.

ACTIONS

1st time   Sing without actions.

2nd time   Instead of singing 'baby', rock folded arms each time.

3rd time   Keep 'baby' action. Instead of singing 'cold', make coughing noise.

4th time   Keep previous actions. Instead of singing 'chest', tap chest.

5th time   Keep all previous actions. Instead of singing 'rubbed', rub chest.

6th time   Keep all previous actions. Instead of singing 'camphorated oil', hold nose.

44 The music man

Leader I am a music man,
I come from far away,
And I can play.
All What can you play?
Leader I play piano.
All Pi-a, pi-a, pi-a-no,
Piano, piano,
Pi-a, pi-a, pi-a-no,
Pi-a, piano.

Leader I am a music man . . .
All What can you play?
Leader I play the big drum.
All Boom-di, boom-di, boom-di-boom,
Boom-di-boom, boom-di-boom,
Boom-di, boom-di, boom-di-boom,
Boom-di, boom-di-boom.
Pi-a, pi-a, pi-a-no,
Piano, piano,
Pi-a, pi-a, pi-a-no,
Pi-a, piano.

Leader I am a music man . . .
All What can you play?
Leader I play the trumpet.
All Toot-ti, toot-ti, toot-ti-toot,
Toot-ti-toot, toot-ti-toot,
Toot-ti, toot-ti, toot-ti-toot,
Toot-ti, toot-ti-toot.
Boom-di, boom-di, boom-di-boom *etc*.
Pi-a, pi-a, piano *etc*.

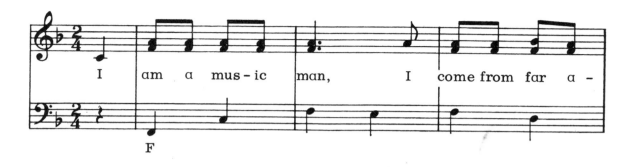

Chorus (repeat as needed)

Pi - a, pi - a, pi - an - o, Pi - an - o,

C7

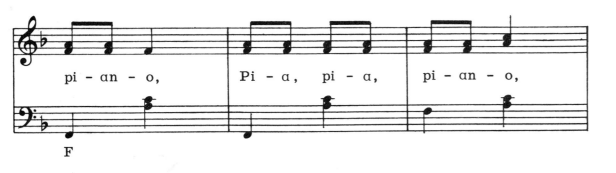

pi - an - o, Pi - a, pi - a, pi - an - o,

F

Last time

Pi - a, pi - an - o. -o.

C7   F   F

ACTIONS

One person takes the leader's part, everyone joining in for 'What can you play?' and for the chorus, with actions.

Choose other instruments to imitate.

45 Oh, we can play on the big bass drum

Oh, we can play on the big bass drum,
And this is the music to it;
Boom, boom, boom goes the big bass drum,
And that's the way we do it.

Oh, we can play on the tambourine,
And this is the music to it;
Chink, chink, chink goes the tambourine,
Boom, boom, boom goes the big bass drum,
And that's the way we do it.

Oh, we can play on the castanets . . .
Click, clickety-click go the castanets . . .

Oh, we can play on the triangle . . .
Ping, ping, ping goes the triangle . . .
Ting Ting Ting

Oh, we can play on the old banjo . . .
Tum, tum, tum goes the old banjo . . .

Shake
tap   wooden blocks

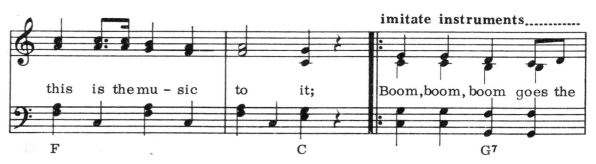
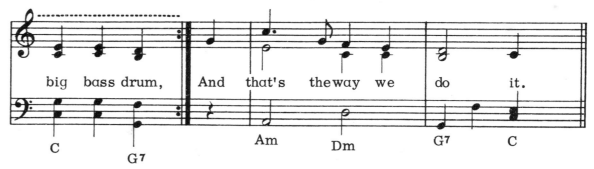

drum   tambourine   castanets   triangle

ACTIONS

With each additional verse, imitate the new instrument first, followed by all the others, working backwards to the first mentioned.

Add as many other instruments as you can manage.

46 One finger, one thumb, keep moving

One finger, one thumb, keep moving,
One finger, one thumb, keep moving,
One finger, one thumb, keep moving,
We'll all be merry and bright.

One finger, one thumb, one arm, keep moving . . .

One finger, one thumb, one arm, one leg,
  keep moving . . .

One finger, one thumb, one arm, one leg,
  one nod of the head, keep moving . . .

One finger, one thumb, one arm, one leg,
  one nod of the head, stand up, sit down,
  keep moving . . .

One finger, one thumb, one arm, one leg,
  one nod of the head, stand up, turn round,
  sit down, keep moving . . .

ACTIONS

Start the song quietly, sitting down. The action builds up
with each verse. Keep up a continuous movement throughout
each verse.

One fin-ger, one thumb, keep mov - ing, One

F

fin-ger, one thumb, keep mov - ing, One fin-ger, one thumb, keep

mov - ing, We'll all be mer-ry and bright.

C7   F

47 I jump out of bed in the morning

I jump out of bed in the morning,
I jump out of bed in the morning,
I jump out of bed in the morning,
I hope it's a very nice day.

I jump out of bed and stretch myself
   in the morning (3 times)
I hope it's a very nice day.

I jump out of bed and stretch myself
   and step in the bath in the morning
   (3 times) . . .

. . . and wash myself in the morning

. . . and dress myself in the morning

. . . and brush my teeth in the morning

. . . and comb my hair in the morning

. . . and eat my toast in the morning

. . . and wave goodbye in the morning

. . . and walk to school in the morning

Beginning of verse 2

I jump out of bed and stretch my-self in the morn - ing,(etc.)

F

ACTIONS

These are as indicated by the words of the song – jump, stretch, step in the bath, wash oneself, and so on.

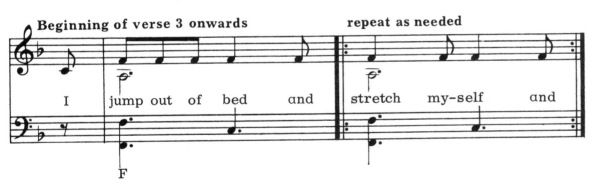

Beginning of verse 3 onwards   **repeat as needed**

I jump out of bed and stretch my-self and

F

step in the bath in the morn - ing, I jump out of bed (etc.)

48 My hat it has three corners

My hat it has three corners,
Three corners has my hat,
And had it not three corners,
It would not be my hat.

hat   three   corners

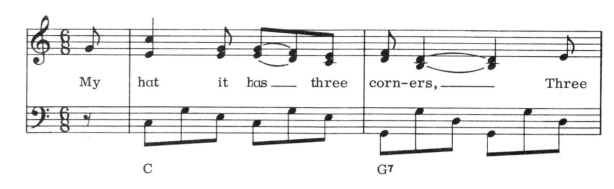

My hat it has ___ three corn-ers, ___ Three

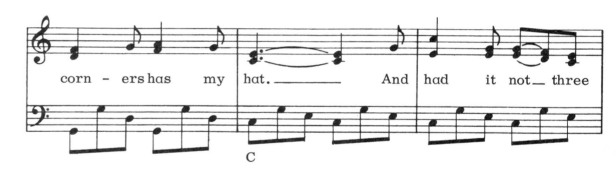

corn - ers has my hat. ___ And had it not ___ three

corn-ers, ___ It would not be my hat. ___

ACTIONS

1st time Sing without actions.

2nd time Instead of singing 'hat', touch top of head each time.

3rd time Keep the 'hat' actions. Instead of singing 'three', hold up three fingers each time.

4th time Keep the 'hat' and 'three' actions. Instead of singing 'corners', raise an elbow each time.

Words and music: Based on an Italian song

49 A-tisket, a-tasket

A-tisket, a-tasket,
A green and yellow basket,
I wrote a letter to my love
And on the way I dropped it.
I dropped it, I dropped it,
And on the way I dropped it.
A little girl picked it up
And put it in her pocket.

ACTIONS

As the group sits singing in a circle, someone walks round outside and quietly drops a letter behind a singer, who then jumps up and – running the other way – tries to beat the 'postman' back to his place. If he succeeds, he becomes the new postman.

50 Have you any bread and wine?

Have you any bread and wine?
    We are the Rovers.
Yes, we have some bread and wine,
    For we're the Guardian Soldiers.

Shall we have a glass of wine?
    We are the Rovers.
One glass of it you'll not have,
    For we're the Guardian Soldiers.

We shall send for the red-coat men,
    We are the Rovers.
What care we for the red-coat men?
    For we're the Guardian Soldiers.

We shall send for the blue-coat men,
    We are the Rovers.
What care we for the blue-coat men?
    For we're the Guardian Soldiers.

Are you ready for a fight?
    We are the Rovers.
Yes, we're ready for a fight,
    For we're the Guardian Soldiers.

Shoot! Bang! Fire!

ACTIONS

Form two groups and sing half a verse each in turn. While your group is singing, march towards the others and back again.

The last three words are shouted, with actions.

51 Sally Saucer

Little Sally Saucer,
Sitting in the water,
Rise, Sally, rise,
Wipe out your eyes.
Turn to the east
And turn to the west
And point to the one
That you like best!

ACTIONS

'Sally' performs the actions inside a circle made by the others, who sing the song as they move round her. She turns in the opposite direction, keeping her eyes covered until the last word. Whoever she is pointing to then goes into the circle as the new Sally.

Instead of 'Sally', the name of the person in the middle can be sung.

52 The no-laugh race

Now the no-laugh race is about to start.
Stand face to face, three inches apart.
Just stand there and stare and stare.
Nobody laugh now, don't you dare!

Wiggle your ears, wiggle your nose.
Wearing eyebrows? Wiggle those.
But if anyone giggles, out he goes!
The laugher is the loser, out he goes!

Now we're down to the last sad face.
He's the winner of the no-laugh race!

Words and music: Dr Seuss
Piano accompaniment: Eugene Poddany

Wig-gle your ears, wig-gle your nose. Wear-ing eye-brows?

G   C   G

Wig-gle those. But if an-y-one gig-gles, out he goes! The

A7   D7   G   C

Finale

laugh-er is the los-er, out he goes! Now we're down to the

D7   G

last sad face. He's the win-ner of the no-laugh race!

C   D7   G

ACTIONS

This is an elimination contest. Stand face to face in pairs and sing the first four lines. As you sing the next four lines, try to make your partner laugh.

Laughers fall out and sing; survivors make new pairs until one is left the winner.

53 The grand old Duke of York

Oh, the grand old Duke of York,
He had ten thousand men,
He marched them up to the top of the hill
And he marched them down again.

And when they were up, they were up,
And when they were down, they were down,
And when they were only half way up,
They were neither up nor down.

Oh, the grand old Duke of York,
He had ten thousand men,
They beat their drums to the top of the hill
And they beat them down again.

Oh, the grand old Duke of York,
He had ten thousand men,
They waved their flags to the top of the hill
And they waved them down again.

Oh, the grand old Duke of York,
He had ten thousand men,
They played their pipes to the top of the hill
And they played them down again.

Oh, the grand old Duke of York,
He had ten thousand men,
They fired their guns to the top of the hill
And they fired them down again.

up, And when they were down, they were down, And

D7   A7   D7

ACTIONS

In the first verse, marching is shown by finger movements; in later verses, actions are as illustrated below. Chorus movements are bobbing up and down.

when they were on - ly half-way up, They were neith - er up nor down.

G   C   G   D7   G

beat the drum

wave the flag

play the pipes

fire the gun

54 Did you ever see a lassie?

Did you ever see a lassie,
A lassie, a lassie,
Did you ever see a lassie
Go this way and that?
Go this way and that way
And this way and that way,
Did you ever see a lassie
Go this way and that?

Did you ever see a laddie?

Did you ever see a postman?

Did you ever see a policeman?

Did you ever see a teacher?

Did you ever see a funny clown?

this way and that way And this way and that way, Did you

D7 G D7 G

While the first half of the verse is sung, one person shows an action to the others. During the second half of the verse, everybody imitates this action.

ev - er see a lass - ie Go this way and that?

D7 G

55 Can you tell me?

Can you tell me, can you tell me
What the typists are doing?
They are tapping, they are tapping,
So I will tap too.

Can you tell me, can you tell me,
What the window cleaners are doing?
They are wiping, they are wiping,
So I will wipe too.

Can you tell me, can you tell me,
What the tailors are doing?
They are sewing, they are sewing,
So I will sew too.

Can you tell me, can you tell me,
What the pop singers are doing?
They are prancing, they are prancing,
So I will prance too.

Can you tell me, can you tell me,
What the grand-dads are doing?
They are nodding, they are nodding,
So I will nod too.

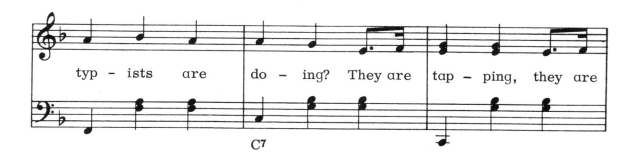

ACTIONS

Divide into two groups, one singing the question and the other the answer.
Everybody joins in the action while the music is repeated.